The Power Within Me

Dear Megan,

Use your Power of Choice Everyday!

Annice

The Power Within Me

The road back home to the *real* you

Annice E. Fisher

Copyright © Dr. Annice E. Fisher 2020. Published in 2020 by BEE FREE Publishing.

All rights reserved.

This book or any portion thereof may not be reproduced or used in any manner whatsoever without the express written permission of the author except for the use of brief quotations in a book review.

ISBN: 978-1-7353001-1-5

20 21 22 23 LSC 10 9 8 7 6 5 4 3 2 1

Table of Contents

Dedication 1

Introduction: The tug-of-war in your spirit 3

Asking: What's going on inside of me? 13

Chapter 1: Recognizing when getting unstuck goes beyond affirmations and mantras 15

Chapter 2: Discerning the two dominant voices in your head 21

Chapter 3: Learning how to regulate your power: The mindset-emotion-behavior pathway 27

Assessing: How am I using my power? 35

Chapter 4: Going deeper into your patterns and defaults .. 37

Chapter 5: Identifying and uprooting external validation . 43

Chapter 6: Staying consistent and managing distractions 55

Accepting: Owning the power within me 63

Chapter 7: Believing in the highest version of yourself 65

Chapter 8: Welcoming the real you 73

Acknowledgements 77

Appendix 79

Glossary of Terms 80

About the Author 82

Dedication

*To my first love: Thank you for guiding me back home to the **real** me. It was always about the mission.*

*To the reader: May you use your power to come back home to the **real** you.*

Introduction: The tug-of-war in your spirit

The real truth behind the smile

Sometimes you feel like no one understands the **real** you or the tug-of-war that is going on inside of you. On the outside, everything looks perfect. Good job, check. Nice house, check. Recognition in your profession, check. A constant chorus of people telling you how great you are, check. Yet your inner voice rings louder and louder with every compliment, *"you're not living up to your full potential, why aren't you using your gifts, why are you running*?" You know that you want to live up to your full potential, but you can't seem to take the leap. Deep down inside you want to listen to your inner voice and ditch the neatly manicured life. Yet each time you try to take the leap towards living up to your full potential, you get pulled back into the vortex of your status quo. It's gotten to the point where you don't know what else to do because your old bag of tricks is not working. The scriptures, mantras, and daily affirmation texts seem to have lost their power to kickstart your momentum. You want to change, but you can't. You feel stuck.

Everyone in your circle looks at you and sees a picture perfect life, yet inside you feel a lack of peace from your invisible inner voice constantly reminding you of your stagnation. The reality is, this isn't *your* picture perfect life because you are not living as the highest version of yourself. The highest version of yourself is the **real** you. It is a state of being that stems from the belief that you are enough and fully capable of using your unique talents and gifts for a greater purpose. For some, this greater purpose could mean changing careers, becoming an entrepreneur, or maintaining a healthy lifestyle. While individual motivations may differ, pursuing the highest version of yourself results in living from a place of comfort, trust, and love, where your mindset, emotions, and behaviors coexist peacefully. This internal harmony allows you to freely use your talents without second-guessing yourself. Your spirit feels at rest because you're channeling your power towards trusting yourself, rather than living from the routinized fear-based expectations of others.

You may have written about the highest version of yourself in your journal or shared it with a few friends and family. You may also have some regrets about sharing it with them, because their reactions to your vulnerability exacerbated your lack of peace and loneliness. The very people that you thought would support you, may have misunderstood why you would disrupt your picture perfect life, or misjudged your calling to live as the highest version of yourself. The negative Nancy comments like, *"Why do you believe that you have this calling?"* or *"You've changed, you are not like us anymore,"* plant seeds of fear and doubt in your mind that trigger your stagnation. So when people ask you, "how are you doing?," you choose to suppress your inner voice, smile and respond, "I'm doing good," all the while descending deeper into a lonely sunken place.

Despite these feelings you persist in your ability to come up for air, and choose to find out what's preventing you from taking action towards living in the highest version of yourself. That's the reason you picked up this book, to get support with figuring out what's going on within you.

This is YOUR time

You picked up this book at the right time in your life. **You will overcome** the fab four of fear and figure out the root of what's actually holding you back. The shouldas, couldas, wouldas, and can'ts of your mind form the foundation of fear-based thinking and self-limiting beliefs that keep you trapped in a cookie cutter life and stifle your voice and potential. Lately, you've felt called to ditch the fab four of fear and jump on a new train, one that leads you to a greater sense of purpose and fulfillment, one that allows your gifts to manifest the ***real*** version of you that you've been dreaming about. Together, we will hit fast forward and pass the powerlessness that fills your mind and spirit with fear of the many things that could go wrong. No more being confined to doubtful thoughts that keep you bound to living as a lower and less happy version of yourself.

*Are you ready to free the **real** you?* I think you are. Want to know how I know? You bought this book which means you are ready to get unstuck. Here's a little trick: if you find yourself getting distracted and wanting to close down, ask *"why is it important for me to be present with this book at this moment in my life?"* Use that answer to ground you and reset your focus. Write down the answer on a post-it note and stick it inside of the book. Use the post-it messages to help you stay motivated along your journey.

Your road to discovering the power within you

You have everything you need inside of you to manifest the highest version of yourself. Power begins on the inside, and you are about to tap into yours in this book. Each chapter will guide you through a consciousness-raising process to discover and reclaim the power within you. Be sure to have your journal handy as you make your way through the book, and be ready to write and reflect on any revelations that come up for you.

First Stop: Promise to Be Honest

This book is about breaking up with fear and doubt and walking in your full power. It's about using your mindset, emotions, and behaviors to live as the highest version of self, releasing the lower vibrations that keep you trapped and playing it safe. In order to let go of the lesser version of yourself and bring out all that beautiful power buried down inside of you,

you have to make yourself a promise. Promise yourself that you will be honest when you answer the questions in this book, **every single time**. To be dishonest is to cheat yourself, stifle your growth, and waste your money. The golden rule of this book is: no judging yourself. View your honest moments as learning moments, too. Judgement will send you back into a corner, leading you to close the book and wind up back at square one. We ain't got time for that; lives depend on you moving forward in your gifts. You chose to investigate your inner voice at this time for a reason, so don't waste your headspace living in negative energy. Every time you want to judge yourself, reframe the thought to, "what am I learning about myself?" This signals a gentler way for your mind to accept new information.

Second Stop: Know the Road Map

In your journey through this book, I will walk you through how to use consciousness-raising strategies to get unstuck. This experience will allow you to get to know yourself on a deeper level and be more thoughtful about how you interact with yourself. The 4-step consciousness-raising process involves ***choice, presence, self-awareness, and intentionality.*** Developing a deeper consciousness starts with:

1. The ***choice*** of how you want to use your power;
2. Your decision then creates a level of ***presence*** to listen to the voices in your mind and find out what's stopping you from moving forward;
3. Using this ***self-awareness***, you can dig up the roots of what has you stuck;
4. And finally ***intentionally*** using hands-on techniques can help you to remove anything that stands in the way of your progression. If it takes you away from the highest version of self, it has to go.

You'll put this process to use in each section of the book as you journey towards reclaiming your power. You will begin in Phase I by Asking: "What's going on inside of me?"; Phase II is about Assessing: "How am I using my power?"; and finally in Phase III, Accepting: Owning the power within me.

Third Stop: Meet Your Companions for the Ride

Personal work is often done alone. This sometimes creates the feeling of isolation and shame as you peel back the layers to unveil the core of your authentic self. There is power in collective vulnerability and healing that occurs within a community. To ensure that you experience the benefits of community throughout this journey, your two new friends, Amina and Grace are here to ride along with you and exemplify the power of the consciousness-raising steps and techniques in each chapter.

Amina

On the outside, people see Amina as someone full of love and inspiration. She is everyone's go-to girl and mentor. She's always making time to care for and support her friends and family. Amina is also an avid social media scroller, constantly posting religious scriptures into her IG stories to motivate her growing number of followers. No one would think she has a deep internal struggle with believing the motivational mantras that she shares with others. Yet, Amina finds herself shying away from the bold dreams and revelations she's received about her calling. Some of her inaction comes from online distractions and her habit of secretly competing with those on her Facebook timeline. Another part of her stagnation stems from the experience of being judged when she shared her hopes and dreams with family. Their judgement planted the seeds of doubt that turned into a forest full of trees by the time Amina turned 30. Perhaps one of the most detrimental seeds that grew was a practice of self-deception; she was secretly living one way, (in a lesser version of herself) and telling herself and others something different (putting on the mentor role for the outside world). Amina didn't want her family to think she was "doing too much" or "trying to live a big life," so she let the seeds grow. Her weight also grew, along with the seeds, from the use of food to suppress the nudges from her inner divinity, whispering the call to live as the highest version of herself. The more she ignored the whispers to live out those bold dreams, the more her weight became a see-saw of losing and gaining pounds.

Over time, Amina's belief in herself became so low that her only comfort came from food and being a mentor to others. Mentorship allowed her to deflect the focus from herself and show up as the self- sacrificing servant to others. Food was the one and only thing that made her feel full; it didn't judge her, and she always felt good when she was around it. But Amina can't even think about living any of her dreams to their full potential because the number on the scale has diminished her inner light. Because she got a high from mentoring people, Amina was able to convince herself that she could bypass digging deeper to understand how she ended up living as a lower version of herself. If she focused on others, she wouldn't have to explore the deeper reasons for her weight fluctuations, fears of judgment, and feelings about living from a place of doubt. Since Amina didn't want anyone to see her sweat, she intensified her inspiration of others so people wouldn't figure out her personal struggles. Now approaching 35, she's tired of lacking internal peace, battling with her weight, and secretly feeling like an imposter. She's ready to get unstuck. Amina woke up one day and decided, it's time to let the ***real*** me out. This was her inner dialogue:

> *"I want to let out the part of me that's dying to adopt a lifelong healthy lifestyle so I can live out my dreams as the highest version of self, the part of me that has a lot to offer the world but can't because of my health concerns, the part of me that wants to prove to everyone that looks down on me because I'm overweight, that I can do it. I need to prove to myself that I can tackle this weight, that I can be who I want to be and live from the same light that I give to others. I am tired of the ups and downs. I want the stability of living as an authentic version of myself that is committed to a healthy lifestyle."*

Grace

Grace is the friend and colleague you call when you need to think of something new. She is a closet creative who would never use *that* word to describe herself, despite the natural talent propelling her career. With each move she made across the country, she collected more and more accolades and bolstered her reputation as a powerful woman for innovation. While Grace loved moving around to launch new initiatives, she often struggled with accepting her gifts, a struggle that dates back to her childhood when kids called her the "teacher's pet" because she won many of the class contests. As she aged in her career, similar echoes came from her colleagues who often loved her to her face, but felt threatened by her talent. For every achievement, she dealt with the growing distance between her and her friends. This caused an internal conflict with her ability to fully accept the power of her gift. In Grace's words,

"I speak the new ideas and catchy phrases that I hear from my spirit and it sticks with people. Those words lead my supporters to believe that I can heal, design, and sell to any audience. I can't help who I am. It comes naturally to me."

As her career progressed, Grace grew more interested in using her skills to serve her inner purpose: using her words to be a change agent. She realized the positive impact that words had on her, from those spoken by her mentors, to those by her favorite authors who guided her through life's transitions. She started to feel a tug to share her lessons learned and innovation strategies in a blog. However, she doubted that people would read her work because she was not a trained journalist or an established writer. Besides, she felt like she didn't fit the "creative mold," with no quirky style, cute thick-rimmed glasses, or familiarity with social media. Still, Grace's friend encouraged her to take the baby step and create a blog. As serendipity would have it, at the end of several meetings, colleagues also began to ask Grace, "did you ever think about writing a book?" Many of them told her "you've been in the game too long, and it is time to share your secret sauce with others." Even in the midst of their encouragement, it was hard for Grace to silence the voices from the childhood taunts and old co-workers' gossip.

A year ago, Grace managed to bypass the sea of doubts and fears to start a blog that helps entrepreneurs pitch new ideas to clients. However, she continued to let the doubts keep her bound to the worries of what others would say and stopped short of calling herself a writer. The revenue generated from her blog and freelance coaching almost superseded the salary of her day job. She still struggles to admit that she loves her blogging and coaching business more than her day job. As more clients ask her, "when are you going to write the book and call yourself an entrepreneur," she brushes them off with, "I'm not a writer, I do this on the side." Grace feels stuck between what she *wants* to do and what others will *say* about what she does. Feeling unsettled about her next steps and the growing whispers from her inner voice to be true to her calling of using her words to be a change agent, Grace knew it was time to get unstuck. She was tired of being controlled by everyone's voice but her own, saying one thing and doing another. She knows that if she gets underneath her own block, it will deepen her blogging and freelance work with clients. She has so much to say to the world and is ready to let it out. If she can only get past the sea of doubts…

Now it's your turn

You've met your passengers, so now introduce yourself. Take a few moments to write and reflect on your story using these prompts:

1. What is one area in your life where you feel stuck? You will apply the 4-step consciousness-raising process to this area at the end of each chapter.

2. What would success or positive change in this area mean to you? Achieving this goal will allow you to manifest the highest version of yourself.

Ultimately, the tug-of-war is about the power of choice

The motivation for this book came from being surrounded by many Aminas and Graces, very talented people on the outside who looked like they had everything all together, yet internally struggled with the crippling effects of fear and doubt. Like you and many others, they grappled with stepping into the highest version of themselves to **let the real me** out. Remember this: you are not alone. Keep this in mind when fear tries to eat away at your courage to stay on this journey.

Fear wants you to continue using your power and choice to erect inauthentic versions of yourself. Somewhere along life's journey, we developed these self-protective mechanisms to feel safe when we received messages that being our **real** selves was not enough. Famous Harvard psychologists Bob Kegan and Lisa Lahey described this process as developing an immune system to protect oneself from perceived harm. The-tug-of-war in your spirit seeks to take your self-protective systems off autopilot so you can redirect the *current* you back home to the **real** you. Throughout this journey, you'll have a plethora of opportunities to use your power and choice to align with the highest version of yourself which is the **real** you. The moment you start to consistently use your gifts while living in the highest version of yourself, things start shifting to align with your bold purpose. When this happens, do not apologize for what you do well or hide your abilities. You were born to share your talents with the world. This is the reason the tug-of-war hit you so strongly, your spirit could no longer handle you living below your full potential. It could no longer handle dimming your light out of fear of other's thinking that you are "doing too much" for wanting to be a better version of yourself. When you let your light shine, you give others permission to shine, too. That's why we've got to get behind what's going on inside of you. We'll start with a topic that everyone shies away from: what to do when your daily affirmation texts, instagram memes, and New Age mantras stop working. There is a reason why they are shooting blanks…getting unstuck is an inside-out job.

Asking: What's going on inside of me?

"No matter where you are on your journey, that's exactly where you need to be. The next road is always ahead."

Oprah Winfrey

Chapter 1: Recognizing when getting unstuck goes beyond affirmations and mantras

When the old bag of tricks stop working

Many of us love our daily affirmation texts and self-help Instagram accounts, but let's be real, they do not always give us the swift kick in the butt that we need to get going. Do not let guilt or shame overwhelm you if you read your religious scripture or affirmations, but do not feel moved to change. When that happens, I'm challenging you to honor yourself in that moment and get curious about the real reason why you're not moved by the message. Your immobility is a sign that you need to pause and go within. It is a sign that your spirit (aka the *divinity within you*) is blocked. When your spirit is ignored and needs to get your attention it issues a "stuck order." A "stuck order" calls out the internal struggle that occurs when you are not paying attention to your inner voice; it is the cry of your spirit to shake you out of stagnation and the cycle of poor, un-affirming choices. Before starting the excavation process to figure out what is going on within, you first need to acknowledge your spirit's "stuck order." Don't panic. You are right where you're supposed to be for this part of your life's journey. Together, we will get you unstuck. But first, let's look at how Amina tried to address the same issue.

Amina's road led to a dead-end

Amina is the motivation queen. From the inspirational messages hanging throughout her home, to the affirmation texts, daily quotes, and self-help

Instagram memes popping up in her notifications, she lives in mantra overflow. She hoped the diversity of daily reminders would keep her spirit centered and uplifted to live as the highest version of herself. Well, that didn't actually come to fruition. I wish I could tell you that every time Amina walks through her house or scrolls on her phone that she swells up with a burst of inspiration. The honest answer is, she barely looks at them for self-motivation, but she readily uses the messages to motivate others. Amina's perpetual doubt in her ability to overcome her weight challenges created a mental block that prevented her from internalizing the multiple sources of motivation. Her attempts to override her mental block failed to work because her internal validation bank account, her ability to believe that she is enough and capable, was already too low. Years of fear and doubt had chipped away at her confidence and eroded her ability to believe she could conquer her goals. She looks at her "Believe in your Dreams" iPhone wallpaper over 30 times a day yet stops short of taking action to bring that message to life. Why can't she take the full leap? What's blocking the mantra overflow from working? What is preventing her from taking action when she reads the memes from her favorite Instagram self-help guru? Amina is growing tired. Her bag of tricks no longer works. She is ready to dig deeper to find out why she is stuck.

Instead of feeling encouraged to bring the affirmations she read to life, Amina's "stuck order" from her doubtful mindset caused her to scroll past them or share the message with others instead of use them for their intended purpose, to spur her into action. Rather than be present and look at her "Pray More & Worry Less" sign while using the bathroom, Amina scrolled on her iPhone to see the number of views on her latest Facebook stories. The strength of her fear-based mindset prevented her from shining her light on herself. Now that we've learned more about Amina's story, let's use the 4-step consciousness-raising technique to understand how a "stuck order" may have led your own inspirational plan to a dead-end.

Now, it's your turn

You have to <u>choose</u> to use your power

You have power and choice in every situation. It's up to you to decide if you want to use them. Power comes from within and waits on us to unleash it. We unleash it in two ways, internally and externally. Unleashing internal power is the process of raising your consciousness to purposefully choose mindsets, behaviors, and emotions that lead to the highest version of yourself. It empowers love and trust. Externally we can give our power to others in two ways. The first way is by granting someone formal authority to act on our behalf (for example, the power we give to elected officials). The second and more detrimental way is by handing our power over for external validation, so that we can ***only*** feel powerful when an external source affirms us. This is an ineffective use of power. The key to releasing the power within is to know that you are enough without the need for anything outside of you to affirm that truth. The way you make internal meaning of your emotions, mindsets, and behaviors shapes how you see the external world. How you respond to those interpretations determines whether you act from your internal power or give it away to external validation. I'll say it again, you always have power and you always have choice. The first step is to realize that you have the power within. Choosing to use it brings you further into consciousness.

You have to honor the <u>present</u> moment

The next step requires "presence," a "being in the moment," that allows you to honor that this is exactly where you are supposed to be. The whispers of your inner voice act as signals from the *divinity within you* trying to get your attention. It's saying, "hey Sis, it's time for us to have a talk." Many block out the signals by, self-medicating the uneasiness away with alcohol, food, drugs, relationships and other avoidance techniques. *Choose* to investigate the signals. Once you make that choice, don't feel bad about the disconnect between what an affirmation calls for and your lack of movement, it happens to many, including Amina, you, and me. This presence of mind generates honesty within yourself that allows you to get to the heart of the matter.

You have to increase your <u>self-awareness</u>

We are all wired both similarly and differently. There are a variety of reasons that contribute to what happens when you read a religious text or affirmation and do not feel moved to act on the message. Self- awareness helps us to understand our reactions. One of the main causes of inaction is that your mind doubts what you see. The moment your eyes register a motivational message, you say "I don't believe that can happen for me." One layer deeper your subconscious mind is saying, "I don't have the power to make that happen for me." We use affirmations, religious texts and mantras to motivate us to act. No one intends to look at them and not feel motivated to do something different. Anytime you don't take that action, it is a sign that something is going on in your internal validation system. This system is where you draw on your internal sources of power, value, and worth. What enables you to act on a scripture, daily quote, or affirmation is a mindset that believes you can bring that statement to life, something inside that says "I got the goods (internal validation) to make this happen." Thus, when a doubtful mindset meets an affirmation, daily quote or mantra, mental blocks become apparent and inaction can result. Self-awareness enables you to pay attention to this dynamic.

You have to deploy yourself <u>intentionally</u>

Your spirit, aka the *divinity within you*, acts as internal checks and balances. When you act contrary to the highest version of yourself, your spirit sends signals to get you back on track. Your everyday decisions determine whether you effectively or ineffectively use your internal power. You have the power to determine whether you want to internalize or ignore the inspirational messages. Manifesting the mantra is influenced by the state of your inner world and your ability to recognize the power within you.

When we pause to read an affirmation yet remain unable to act on it, fear and doubt are inevitably present. The best thing to do is to acknowledge and accept that this is exactly where you are supposed to be on your journey. Acknowledge *without* judgment. Use this as a learning moment about your power. How you use your internal power (mindset, behaviors, and emotions) determines whether trust drives you to action, or doubt maintains your status quo.

Key takeaway

Affirmations, Instagram memes, religious texts, and daily quotes are great tools, yet sometimes we need a little bit more when our spirit issues a "stuck order." A lack of consciousness on how you use your internal power can block you from taking action when reading an affirmation text. Amina has mantras in abundance, but she couldn't get past the *divinity within her* trying to get her attention. The tug-of-war in our spirits shakes us back to reality, calling forth a reckoning with the present moment. Many ignore the shaking and suffer from living as a lesser version of themselves. It is time to specifically address what's going on inside that leads you to live below your full potential. The first step is to ask yourself: "What can I learn from my inability to enact change from my daily affirmations?" From there, you have to make the choice to become more present, using that self-awareness to make more intentional choices. You have to make the choice to use your internal power to access the highest version of yourself.

Now that you know nothing is wrong with you and understand this is a phenomenon that happens to everyone, we can start to tackle the deeper issues feeding your inability to internalize affirmations and take action. Navigating the interplay of our internal power and external manifestation can be challenging; however, having the courage to explore the "stuck order" is the first step towards freeing your mind and deploying the highest version of yourself from trust and love. Recognizing that you have power and choice in every situation sets the ball in motion to disentangle doubt's grip on your life. Now it's time to examine the voices in your head that drive doubt's car and prevent you from gassing up on your daily affirmations, memes, daily quotes, and mantras.

Chapter 2: Discerning the two dominant voices in your head

The voices in your head determine your path

Just like the GPS in a car tells you where to turn, the voices in your head direct your life. If you put in the wrong direction, you end up off course. The GPS takes its orders from the information you enter into the system. Similarly, your behaviors respond to the voices in your head. You must be intentional with how you allow your thoughts to direct your behaviors. When we live our lives on autopilot for too long, we end up with the "stuck orders" we discussed in the last chapter. This chapter focuses on taking yourself off autopilot in order to listen to the voices in your head and discern what keeps you stuck and living below your full potential. With this curiosity, let's jump into why you need to become friends with *some* of the voices in your head.

Any sound psychiatrist, therapist, or coach will tell you to listen to the voices in your head because they help diagnose what is actually going on in your life. Two dominant voices battle with each other in directing your life: the voice of love and trust and the voice of fear and doubt. Each voice seeks to control your power. These voices are so powerful that they are able to create your reality. Whether you choose to listen to the voice of love and trust or of fear and doubt can send you in directions that can create either benefits or losses. As described in the introduction, our daily goal is to choose the path which leads us to living as the highest version of ourselves. The voice of love and trust depicts your world from a mindset of abundance. It lets you know that you are enough and you are capable of handling anything that comes your way. This causes an unwavering belief in yourself and your decisions. On the other hand, the voice of fear and doubt depicts your world through a mindset of scarcity. It smothers your sense of self and stifles your inner power by keeping you ruminating on thoughts of unbelief. These twins, fear and doubt, threaten your gifts and relegate you to the lowest version of self. Fear and love cannot coexist, neither can *trust and doubt* be friends. To illustrate the battle of the voices, let's take a look at what's going on in Grace's head.

The battle of the voices: Grace edition

In the introduction, you learned that Grace is torn between becoming a full-time writer or leaving her current position as a well-established innovation professional. She is trying to figure out how to get unstuck so she can move towards her calling; to use her words for social change. Grace is at a decision point between her current career and her true purpose. Does she stay on the current track to advance as an innovation C-Suite executive or use her skills more globally and across all sectors as a writer? Fear continues to grip Grace as she takes steps towards her purpose through her successful blog and coaching business, yet still avoids calling herself a writer. If she could resolve her internal battles, she'd be able to see that her gifts as an innovator *and* communicator transcend any one specific identity. Once Grace understands this truth, she can place less emphasis on the title of "Writer" and more on becoming someone that uses words for social change. Unless Grace turns off the autopilot, she'll continue to feel torn, letting the voice of fear and doubt overpower the voice of love and trust. Until she starts dealing with the fears and doubts that came from being teased as a child and from her co-workers' gossip, Grace will continue to waver between trusting her gifts and doubting her skills as a writer. If Grace doesn't confront her internal battle, she will continue to hold distorted perceptions of her reality that leave her locked out of enjoying the transition into the highest version of herself. Her mind will continue to be hijacked by fear and doubt unless she deals with her need for validation from those around her. She will remain unable to see that when she practices trust and moves on instinct, people embrace her words and advice. In order for Grace to build her trust, she needs to address why she is afraid to walk in her own power. Now let's use the 4-step consciousness-raising process to take a deeper look at understanding and discerning the voices in your head that prevent you from living in the highest version of yourself.

Now, it's your turn

You have the power to choose

You have power and choice in every situation. It's up to you to use it. You have the power to redirect the voices in our mind. It is scientifically proven that you cannot control the thoughts that enter your mind. However, you can control how long you let a thought stay and whether you allow fear and doubt to build a house, picket fence, and garden in your mind. Let's look at the default voice that dominates your head.

- The first question you must ask is, "Which voice is loudest in my life?" You can choose whether to let fear and doubt reign supreme or to operate from a place of love and trust.

You have to stay present

Slowing down to answer the question above allows you to be present and to ground yourself in how you naturally use your power. It's like hitting the pause button. In order to effectively monitor the voices in your head, you have to ease off autopilot and focus on what you notice about yourself in this present moment. Adaptive Leadership expert, Ronald Heifetz describes this as "getting on the balcony," the process of slowing down to identify trends. You have to slow down to discern when fear and doubt dominate your thoughts and when love and trust dominate.

- Next, ask yourself: "How am I currently directing my thoughts? Am I going down the pathway of love and trust or fear and doubt?"

Dig deep to increase your <u>self-awareness</u>

Unearthing what's going on in your head will help you discover what keeps you from living as the highest version of yourself. For instance, if we go back to the "stuck order" introduced in Chapter 1, we see that fear-based thinking created the mindset that you could not act on the message in the scripture or affirmation. Similarly, fear and doubt have created a mental block that keeps you from believing that you can reach the highest version of yourself. Let's look at how the voices of fear are active in your own life.

- Ask yourself: What are the top three fear voices that prevent me from living as the highest version of myself (as identified in the introduction)?
- Then go even deeper: "Where did the voices behind these fears come from (parents, colleagues, family, etc.)?"

Deploy yourself with more <u>intentionality</u>

Increasing your self-awareness provides critical information for you to make conscious choices on how to deploy yourself to achieve your desired outcomes. It helps you understand the values and losses associated with each of the voices that guide your life. From here you are able to make an intentional decision on whether to let the fear or doubt remain or reverse them with love and trust.

Here's how to redirect automatic negative thoughts when the voice of fear tells you it's impossible to live as the highest version of yourself:

- Identify the top automatic negative thought (ANT) that pops into your mind when you attempt to live as the highest version of yourself.
- Write the ANT and next to it write Truth of the Matter (TOM). To discover the Truth of the Matter, go back into your history and recall instances where you successfully overcame the ANT.
- Select the top TOM that most powerfully connects to your spirit and overpowers the ANT. This is the TOM that allows you to push past the negative thought and reveal your possibilities. To live as the highest version of yourself. It is simply not enough to identify the ANT, you must replace it with another truth.
- Write the TOM in your cell phone or another place where you can easily access it when the ANT comes back into your head.
- When the ANT returns to your mind, replace it with the TOM.
- Repeat this until the ANT becomes extinct (trust me, it will over time because you have replaced the thought).

Key takeaway

There is a war of voices going on in your head, and you get to choose which one wins. The fight for your highest version of yourself includes winning the battle of love and trust over fear and doubt. Knowing which voice dominates your thinking gives you insight to make different decisions in the moment. Turning down the voice of doubt and turning up trust transforms the distorted realities that run in your mind. Each action you take to become more conscious shuts down the autopilot in your decision-making. This is an essential step towards establishing presence that leads to self-awareness, thus triggering more intentional decisions in the moment. Naming the fears (ANT) that stifle your ability to walk in the highest version of yourself allows you to create specific strategies (TOM) for disrupting that line of thinking. Knowing that you have the power to decide which voice is louder is essential. Give yourself permission every day to become present, become self-aware, and to choose love and trust as the voice that best serves the highest version of yourself.

As we continue the journey to Chapter 3, you will see why it becomes even more important that you remain aware of the voices in your mind and regulate them towards achieving the highest version of yourself. You'll learn that whichever path you choose sets your power in motion. Choose wisely because your exercise of power depends on it.

Chapter 3: Learning how to regulate your power: The mindset-emotion-behavior pathway

"Free your mind and the rest will follow"

While they cannot claim the title of mindset coach or therapist, En Vogue dropped a message of psychological truth with the hook "free your mind and the rest will follow." Any respectable therapist, coach, and psychologist starts every deep examination with "what were you thinking at the time of the incident?" Most religious traditions and New Age movements echo the same sentiment; that enlightenment begins with renewing and mastering the mind. But you don't need En Vogue or a spiritual teacher to tell you that your mindset controls the show. You have a plethora of evidence from your own life. Think about the last time you woke up and a negative thought greeted you as your feet hit the floor. Let's say, the thought was "I'm unhappy in my relationship with my partner." For you it might not be a relationship but rather some other negative thought bringing you down. A negative mindset throws the ball in motion for depressed feelings and sluggish behaviors. That negativity fulfills the prophecy spoken by the voice of fear in your head. Since we know that the mindset sets your emotions and behaviors in motion, this chapter focuses on training your mindset to work for and not against you.

Amina's lifelong challenge to maintain a healthy lifestyle

Amina became overweight at eight years old. The weight surge coincided with being teased by her family for being a kid who loved books. She struggled with her weight throughout her formal schooling years and into her professional career. Before getting to this point, Amina tried every diet fad out there from cabbage soup, to shredding, to weight loss pills; Chinese dieters tea to Weight Watchers. Each of these attempts ended in failure. Her use of food for emotional support created an unhealthy attachment. Although she presented herself as having everything together and being okay with the extra weight, Amina secretly battled dark emotions. Looking in the mirror, Amina often felt sadness and resentment which solidified a mindset that she would always be overweight. She attempted to mask her fear-driven mindset by focusing her time on mentoring others and portraying a false sense of happiness. She was able to do this well, given the amount of mantras that overflowed in all areas of her life. Amina got hit in the face with a hard truth after she attempted to qualify for bariatric sleeve surgery; she failed to meet the pre-qualifying medical conditions to have her insurance cover the costs. She felt defeated as another weight loss door slammed shut. She pondered, "Is this God's way of saying that I need to do the personal work to lose the weight?"

Amina didn't know how she was going to do it, but she made up her mind. She was not going to get any bigger and she was going to lose the weight. After many failed attempts at quick fixes, Amina realized she needed to dig deeper into the cause of her obesity. She began to understand how food became an emotional escape, how she used food to feel full instead living a full life. This choice point helped Amina see just how much fear and food controlled her life, how much food dictated her happiness. With her newfound self-awareness Amina started to make more intentional choices; she hired a trainer and nutritionist to build her a regimen. Choosing trust allowed Amina to shift her mindset about her weight challenges, improve her mood from despair to hope, and shift her actions toward living a healthy lifestyle. Now let's look at how you can regulate your power pathway towards living from your highest version of self.

Regulating the power pathway

As I shared in the last chapter, your choices will predict whether you let the voice of love and trust or fear and doubt direct your life. If fear lays the foundation, then you must process, release, then evict it. Some of my coaching clients will say, "Dr. Annice I do not know if my mindset is in doubt or trust, I tend to exercise caution with my decision making. How can I know which it is?" This is when I get excited and pull out my handy dandy chart, which helps us use our emotions as diagnostic clues about our mindset. Let's look at the *Power and Choice Pathway* chart for a visual depiction of the "Mindset--Emotions--Behaviors" pathway in motion. The left side describes the emotions activated by a mindset of love and trust, the right side identifies those activated by fear and doubt. A love and trust mindset always leads to feelings of peace and compassion which lead to behaviors of bravery and living as the highest version of yourself. A fear and doubt mindset leads to anxiety and resentment which, in turn, lead to status quo, instability, and living as a lesser version of yourself.

The Power and Choice Pathway

Even if you do not know your frame of mind, you can always use your emotions and behaviors as clues for understanding your mindset, and discerning which voice is louder, love and trust or fear and doubt. You can also self-check with these questions:

- Mindset: Do I believe *I am enough* and *capable of handling the task* in front of me?
- Emotions: Do my emotions lead to peace or anxiety?
- Behaviors: Do I exercise bravery or act from the status quo and safety?

Now, for the skeptics reading this text, you might be saying "This sounds all good but what if I am so far in the deep end from having a bad day that I can't even utter these questions?" Then I would say to you, first honor where you are. Don't judge yourself for having a bad day. Honor the present reality, but don't stay in it. Push through to process and release the fear. Remember you have power and choice in every situation and it is up to you to decide to use them. Begin by asking:

- "At this moment, am I using my power to trust myself or doubt myself?" That will trigger the emotional and behavioral aspects of the power pathway. Everyday you get to choose to direct your mindset, behaviors, and emotions towards the highest version of yourself.
- If you find yourself with negative emotions like Amina did, ask yourself: "Where are these emotions coming from?"
- Then ask: "What are the hidden fears and doubts driving those emotions and behaviors?"

Remember: no judging. You are asking these questions to learn more about how you use your power. Let's look at how you can use the 4-step consciousness-raising technique to direct your mindset, emotions, and behavior pathways towards living as the highest version of yourself.

Now, it's your turn

Use <u>choice</u> to regulate your power pathway

Every single day you have to be intentional about your thought life. Throughout Chapters 1-3, we've echoed that sentiment in many different ways. Living life on autopilot is what got you stuck. Getting unstuck requires you to regulate your power towards love and trust. It's okay if you find yourself in fear and doubt. Process those feelings and move toward love and trust. Make it a habit several times a day to pause and ask yourself:

- "How do I want to use my power in this situation? To instill trust or doubt? To create fear or love?"

Use <u>presence</u> to identify trends in your power usage

Once you've identified how you want to use your power, you can do a self-check to determine if you're truly using your power in that way. This is one of the most important steps: to build in time to pause, go within and inquire about the trends of your power usage. Several times throughout the day ask yourself:

- "Am I using my power in the way I intend?"

Allow <u>self-awareness</u> to create the lever for change

You can identify the feelings going on *within* you and the factors in your environment that influence how you use your power. This helps you become more aware of internal and external triggers that prompt or stifle advancement into your highest version" of self. Ask yourself:

- "When does my fear and doubt mindset show up to stifle me from living as the highest version of myself?"
- "When does my love and trust mindset motivate me to live as the highest version of myself?"

It's up to you to become <u>intentional</u> at regulating your power

Now it is time to make a plan to shift your daily mindsets, emotions, and behaviors to walk in love and trust. Fill in the blanks below:

- I plan to do _____ as a clear action to help me live as the highest version of myself.
- I am going to _____ to keep my mindset grounded in love and trust.

Your mindset can kickstart you to live as the highest version of yourself rather than steer your emotions and behaviors away from this goal. Understand that you have power and choice. Make the choice to be guided by love and trust. Create a mental presence to assess what is going on, and use that deeper self-awareness to be more intentional.

Key takeaway

When you free your mind, the rest will follow. Make the commitment to regulate your mindset, emotions, and behaviors. Set your mind on love and trust instead of fear and doubt. Remember, you wield the power to adjust your mindset anytime it derails you down the path to fear. Staying present leads to an awareness that activates your internal checks and balances to monitor all aspects of the chain: mindset, behaviors, and emotions. This is an essential step to not only owning your power, but also believing in yourself and walking in your power.

In this section, you've answered the question, "What's going on inside of me?" Up to now you have discovered that:

1. You are not crazy for being unable to use scriptures or affirmations to activate love and trust to walk in your highest version of self. There is something else going on inside of you that must be explored so you can get free. You have power. You have four tools available to you at all times: choice, presence, self-awareness, and intentionality.
2. There are two voices warring in you to control your emotions and behaviors. They are the voice of love and trust and the voice of fear and doubt. Each one leads to different outcomes---one taking you up and the other taking you down. Knowing which one is driving you most of the time is important to unlocking your potential. You have power in every situation to choose the voice that takes you up to your highest self.
3. Your mindset influences everything, including your emotions and behaviors. Knowing which voice is driving your mindset is key. Constantly being aware of and regulating the pathway is important. Use your current emotions and behaviors as a self-check. You have the power to change your mindset at any time to move towards higher or lower self. It requires making a choice.

With a greater awareness of mindset as a driver and a realistic look at how it either sabotages or aids your aspirations, you can make different decisions. And with a better assessment of the roles played by love and trust, and fear and doubt, you can identify and pull up the roots of the things preventing you from living as the highest version of yourself. Let's assess how you're using your power. We will begin by talking about one area that makes us cringe: going deeper into your patterns and defaults.

Assessing: How am I using my power?

YOU

"Your sickness is from you, but you do not perceive it and your remedy is within you, but you do not sense it. You presume you are a small entity, but within is enfolded the entire Universe. You are indeed the evident book, by whose alphabets the hidden becomes manifest.
Therefore you have no need to look beyond yourself. What you seek is within you, if only you reflect."

Imam Ali (AS)

Chapter 4: Going deeper into your patterns and defaults

Personal mastery is the key to getting unstuck

Let's be honest. Staying the course of love and trust is hard. But I didn't have to tell you that. You knew it before picking up the book and having me repeat this theme over the last 3 chapters. Even so, we find hope in a key universal truth: the remedy is within you. Unfortunately, like Imam Ali says, many times we do not perceive, nor sense, nor realize that within us lies the key to everything that we need. We spend eternity searching and seeking validation from things outside of ourself.

This book seeks to shift your perspective from looking beyond yourself, to examining your internal environment to better understand yourself. Opening the pages of your personal book reveals the "alphabets" or stories that explain the causes of your "sickness" (i.e., self-sabotaging patterns, distractions, external validations). This process of revelation transitions you from seeing yourself as a small entity to an entire Universe, a Universe ripe to manifest all that is needed for you to unapologetically walk as the highest version of yourself. Living as a Universe requires love and trust so you can begin manifesting the unimaginable. But first, we must understand your defaults and patterns.

Understanding your sicknesses will require brutal honesty. Over the next three chapters we are going to explore the defaults and patterns that sabotage your ability to live as your highest self. You will identify the origins of your fear and doubt and the distorted view of yourself that keeps them intact. Operating from fear-based defaults and patterns causes self-sabotage that threatens your progression. In order to obtain personal mastery and "see yourself as the Universe," you need to know how you get in your own way. Let's look back at Grace from Chapter 2. Remember, she's at a transition point of choosing between her career as an innovation professional or moving into her calling to use her words for social change. Fear and doubt has her vacillating between taking the leap and maintaining the status quo. Let's see how her patterns and defaults developed over time.

Grace's fear-based defaults and patterns

The doubtful voices go back to Grace's childhood experience of being teased for her intelligence. This established her initial fear-based thought patterns. Grace believed from an early age that "if you show your full power, people will make fun of you." The taunts throughout her K-12 experience built a firm root in her thinking, "never show too much of yourself " and, "diminish yourself when speaking with friends." This created a pattern of withholding parts of herself from friends and building up internal walls that blocked true intimacy. This continued through her professional experience. Grace's hard work and innovative approaches garnered attention that led to invitations to collaborate that were not afforded to her peers. Yet, with every open door, her friends grew distant and her close relationships diminished. Seeing this play out cemented her initial fear, "if you show up in your full power, then people will leave you." When the covert bullying began at her jobs, she did what she knew best: "diminish part of yourself with colleagues, so they will like you."

Grace's "if, then" fear-based mindset created a distorted view of herself that caused her to see her gifts and skills as both a burden and a blessing. When she viewed them as a blessing and trusted herself as the person called to serve others through innovative problem solving, the opinions of others and her default "if, then" thinking did not matter. Her focus on the task overpowered her fear of rejection from her colleagues. However, her fear-based mindset would kick into gear when she heard the side-eye comments from her peers when her accomplishments were recognized by her supervisor. The feelings of loss in her relationships made her see her gift as a burden. It also solidified her patterns of distancing and diminishing herself after each successful project announcement. Her fear-based mindset clouded her ability to enjoy healthy friendships throughout the course of her achievements. People would often ask Grace, "why didn't you tell us about the great news?" The truth is, Grace's "if, then" thinking prevented her from celebrating herself. Because of this default pattern, Grace rarely felt pure joy with her success.

Unreleased fear-based thinking continued to silently influence Grace, leading her to behave and emote in ways that threatened the very goals that she sought---connection with her peers. Her fear and doubt- based view of self stifled Grace from fully walking in love and trust to her true calling of using her words for social change as an author. Her distorted view of herself stayed intact because she allowed every positive experience to reconfirm her fear of rejection. However, she didn't see that her pattern of diminishing herself and withholding good news worked against her goal to establish intimacy with her peers. This behavior kept Grace from walking in her full power to expand her platform beyond her innovation job to serve more people as a writer. Now let's use the 4-step consciousness-raising techniques to help you go deeper into the defaults and patterns that threaten your progression into your highest version of self.

Now, it's your turn

You have a <u>choice</u> to go deeper

You bought this book because you are tired of your "inner voice" reminding you of being stuck. You know the detrimental effects of living with a distorted view of yourself that sabotages your ability to live as the highest version of yourself. You feel it everyday. Peeling back the layers is a must for you to understand how you are using your power.

- You can begin by asking yourself: "What motivates me to go deeper into my defaults and patterns?"

You have to stay <u>present</u> to interrupt the autopilot of self-sabotage

Making the choice to interrupt self-sabotage creates the learning container for you to become more present in your day-to-day life. Presence allows you to slow down and look for patterns and trends that feed your fear and doubt. Presence gives you an important perspective before taking future action. The process of slowing down will aid you to discern how your current defaults and patterns negatively influence your goals:

- When you slow down, ask: "What are the main defaults and patterns that prevent me from walking as the highest version of myself ? Highlight the pattern that you most want to change.

<u>Self-awareness</u> generates knowledge about the root

Identifying defaults and patterns results in a greater self-awareness of the self-sabotage. It also helps you determine the root of these mindsets, emotions, and behaviors. This knowledge creates leverage for you to detach yourself from unconsciously living on autopilot and to do something about your distorted perception of self.

- For the top default pattern identified above, ask yourself: "What are the internal and external triggers that set off the mindsets, emotions, and behaviors that lead me to self-sabotage?"

<u>Intentionally</u> decide to release the self-sabotage

With this greater sense of self-awareness, you can be more intentional with how you use your power in the world. You can interrupt the patterns you discovered above and create internal checks and balances. You are not in the dark anymore, mindlessly going through life trapped in your self-sabotage. When you decide to live in fear-based defaults, you are making a conscious choice to live as a lesser version of yourself.

- What are the negative costs that fear-based defaults and patterns have on your life? Use these costs to redirect your self-sabotage.

Key takeaway

You can become a master of yourself by raising your consciousness. You choose to be more present by activating an awareness that allows for more intentionality. Personal mastery is the key. We get to personal mastery by taking time to put our behaviors, mindsets, and emotions under a microscope. Once under a microscope we have to discover how and why they developed. Treating yourself with grace during this reflection process is important. These honest portrayals of self helps you discern how your power is compromised by fear-based defaults and patterns. The 4-step consciousness-raising process demonstrates that you have the power to choose to be more present and use your self- awareness to take intentional steps to end defaults and self-sabotage. You have the power and choice to move away from fear and doubt based living to a life based on love and trust. One that allows you to start owning your gifts. One that allows you to start living in your calling. You are now on your way to becoming a master of self. Being able to say "I am on my way to living as a Universe," free from judgment is one of the greatest victories of personal mastery. Knowing how you get in your own way creates a deeper relationship between your mind and your spirit. A deeper relationship with yourself. A more honest relationship that owns and honors your unique being. This is essential to embracing all of you.

Our next step is to understand the roots of your patterns. We will go deeper to understand the factors that keep you from living as the highest version of yourself. There is a story behind why your self- sabotage, defaults and patterns emerged. There's a reason why the autopilot behavior runs deep. It connects back to the root of dependency on external validation that developed earlier in your life.

Chapter 5: Identifying and uprooting external validation

Internal validation, external validation, & power

You've heard it before: much of what impacts you in adulthood dates back to your childhood. Now, this isn't a reason to pick up the phone and yell at the people who raised you. They did the best they could with what they knew how to do. This book is about personal accountability. The reason I'm dedicating the longest chapter in the book to uprooting external validation is because it is the silent killer to living as the highest version of yourself. This chapter will become the turning point on your journey because you will dig up the roots of external validation that feed into the challenges you identified in the previous chapters.

You can use your power to bolster internal validation or depend on external validation. Internal validation draws your source of power, value, and worth from within and honors your intuition. A dependence on external validation threatens your sense of worthiness, leads to emotional instability, and renders *feelings* of powerlessness when the external stimuli is missing.

Craving external validation is the greatest threat to your identity and recognition of the power within you. There is nothing wrong with liking nice things or desiring love from your partner or seeking a promotion--- that is all perfectly normal. The distortion happens when you feel less-than if you do not acquire these external things. Your external power becomes misused when you attach your sense of self to a person, place, or thing. Are you ready to pull up the roots of the external validations that render you powerless to move forward?

We learned affection instead of love

In all likelihood, your dependence on external validation goes back to the messages you learned from those who raised you. Many who struggle with a dependence on external validation have grown up feeling like you were "not enough" unless you acquired accomplishments. Those feelings may have also caused you to feel a lack of genuine love for being the **real** you.

If you struggle with a dependence on external validation, you likely weren't given a definition of love outside of it being something you "do" for another person to "feel" cared for. There are a million ways to define love. I use a combination of M. Scott Peck's definition and my own: love is channelling our mindset, emotions, and behaviors to nurture one's own or another's spiritual growth. While reading bell hooks' iconic *All About Love*, I discovered M. Scott Peck's timeless classic, *The Road Less Traveled*. hooks cited Peck's definition as key to her understanding of love and influential to her trilogy of books on love.

Most of us were taught affection *in place of* love. Affection is a behavior used to show care or to affirm an experience in order to please both the giver and receiver with an external validation. Do you remember how your parents or guardians first responded when you "won" something at school? It was probably a smile, hug or pat on the back accompanied by "I love you" or "I'm so proud of you." As these types of interactions accumulated over childhood, many kids came to crave the *affection* their parents showed towards them for doing something good. This unintentional misuse of affection as love planted the seeds of a validation system based on things external to yourself.

An example of the same childhood interaction fueled by genuine love instead of affection may have looked something like this: Your parents would ask you to tell them about the positive things that you achieved (i.e. winning a spelling bee). You'd explain to them what you did. They'd respond by saying "I'm proud of you" and would let you know that when you believe in yourself and work hard, you can accomplish anything, even if you don't get a reward for it. The real reward is proving to yourself that you can overcome anything. That type of interaction would have nurtured you to see the benefits of winning are about trusting yourself as capable of accomplishing difficult tasks (love). Without explaining the intrinsic benefits of the hard work and reward (love), "I'm proud of you" and "I love you" (affection) becomes unexplained and can create a lifestyle of achievement focused on gaining external validations to feel and hear love. This may have set the ball in motion for your worth to become tied to titles and external things. If I just read your diary in this section, forgive yourself for having a dependence on external validation. Use this as a learning moment to understand why it was so hard for you to uproot external validation. Now that you have the important background, let's see how this dynamic played out in Grace's life.

The miseducation of Grace

Grace's life provides an excellent example of the many faces of external validation. Her anxiety and preoccupation with external validation centered on being liked by others. For her, being smart as a child and successful in her professional life came at the cost of getting teased and losing friendships. Thus, she diminished herself around her peers and family. She lived her life at the mercy of how people felt about her which created anxiety with moving into her calling. Grace feared, "what will people say about me leaving a corporate innovation job to become a writer or change agent?" Her anxiety is a sign that fear and doubt drive her mindset. Again, on the outside, it looks like things are going well, but on the inside, she is constantly afraid of living as her *real* self. However, if you dig deep beyond Grace's initial complaints about the loss and teasing, you will notice a bit of self-deception on her end. She secretly feels more valuable when others validate her and she succeeds. This stems from a childhood where she only heard, "I love you" and received affection from her parents when she excelled at a task. Grace is unlikely to share that truth with others because she doesn't want to face the root of her self-deception. She now has to work extra hard to get back to a healthy sense of self.

Starting her blog was a positive step forward for Grace to strengthen her internal validation. For once, she was not driven by the success of her business or client accolades. Every act Grace takes with her side business builds love and trust that strengthens her internal validation. She's almost ready to take the leap to leave her neatly manicured life to pursue her calling. Next we will apply the 4-step consciousness-raising process to help you to uproot your need for external validation and live as the highest version of yourself.

Now, it's your turn

You have the choice to dig up the root

Let's get right into it. You are going to explore the roots of your power to instill internal validation and decrease your dependence on external validation. Take a moment to go back to your childhood.

- Go back and really think about it: When was the first time you became driven by external validation?
    - How did you learn the habit of performing for affection?

- When was the first time you experienced being driven by internal validation?
    - How did you learn to internally validate yourself?

Explore the <u>presence</u> of both forms of validation in your life

Now, I know you are thinking that this is a lot easier said than done. And you are right, it is difficult to do. Many of us do not realize how much our dependence on external validation drives our lives because we live on autopilot. Slowing down to assess which validation drives your power, is essential for the long-term reclamation of your power. Identify the top 3 strongest forms of external validation that prevent you from living as the highest version of yourself. Fill in the blank below with your external validation. Then, repeat the two statements in each bullet three times each.

- *If I do not have _____ validation in my life, I feel like I am not enough.*
    - *I first developed this mindset when _____.*

- *Dependence on this external validation impacts my self-worth by _____.*
    - *External validation has stifled me from walking in my gifts because _____.*

<u>Self-awareness</u> identifies which validation guides you

Let's get started by figuring out whether internal or external validation drives how you see yourself in both your mind and your heart. This test explores which form of validation drives you the most and informs your self-image. Now, be REALLY honest with these answers. Lying to yourself will only strengthen your self-deception. Being truthful is essential to this process and it lets us know where to target the work.

Validation Test

Circle the top 14 things that drive your personal sense of satisfaction and feelings of love, empowerment, and value. Do not judge yourself, just answer the questions honestly.

Sources of my validation:

1. being chosen by someone to be in a committed relationship
2. using my power and choice to trust myself when making decisions
3. receiving an award for my accomplishments
4. receiving public recognition for accomplishing a hard task
5. believing in a bold purpose and acting on that belief
6. driving a luxury car as my primary mode of transportation
7. speaking up and living in my truth
8. following the Creator's plan for my life
9. receiving daily compliments/constant adoration from colleagues
10. saying no to others when it means compromising my values
11. receiving regular promotions
12. honoring the present moment
13. being intentional with my choices
14. personal satisfaction from accomplishing a hard task
15. receiving likes on my social media posts
16. being seen as an expert in my field
17. being seen as the go-to person
18. using wisdom from life's lessons
19. having a grateful disposition
20. checking in with what I need and giving it to myself
21. honoring my intuition from a non-fear based lens

22. having a title of influence
23. receiving constant adoration from close friends and family
24. being seen as the "smartest person in the room"

Now compare your answers to the key at the end of the book. Did most of your responses fall under internal or external validation? If they mostly fall under internal validation, then that is your power base, according to these areas. If it is mostly external validation, then that is your power base, too. How did you do?

If most of the responses you circled were from external validation, I know that can be difficult to swallow. But let's swallow this big pill so you can start to heal. Owning that you are driven by what others see you do is difficult but don't go beating yourself up. Stop the self-deprecating talk that's on auto-play in your head. I am proud of you for being honest with yourself. I know it stings, and you may want to close this book and curse me out. Don't do it! You just got one step closer to returning to the ***real*** you. We just sucker-punched the lie that told you to believe that your value comes from things outside of you. We ripped off the veil of self-deception that blinded your sight. In essence, ish just got real. So let's keep going. You got this and we are in it together. Look at yourself through a learning lens. Ask: "What did I just learn about myself from this inventory? What makes sense NOW about how I behave that I didn't know 5 minutes ago, before I answered the questions?" Stay in this learning mindset and let's keep going.

<u>Intentionally</u> address your sources of validation

Many of us care what people think and *we care about it way too much*. You've been living with the paradigm of external validation for many years, making it hard to recognize and difficult to uproot. Next, I will walk you through techniques for releasing external validation and strategies for sustaining internal validation.

In one of his last books, *Letting Go: The Pathway to Surrender,* clinical psychiatrist David Hawkins discusses the pathway to releasing the burden of negative emotions that block us from enlightenment. Letting go is a process of letting a negative emotion pass through by releasing small aspects. It also helps you dis-identify with a negative emotion by realizing they come and go. These strategies modify David Hawkins' "letting go" techniques.

Uprooting External Validation

Step 1: Use the top three external validations that you named in the presence step.

- (Repeat for each validation) If I do not have X (fill in the blank with an external validation) in my life, then I feel like I am not enough because _____.

Step 2: Start to release small aspects (images/attachments).

- Can you let go of (because statement 1)? Yes---I can let go of trying to control (because statement 1) because of _____.
- Can you let go of (because statement 2)? Yes---I can let go of trying to control (because statement 2) because of _____.
- Can you let go of (because statement 3)? Yes---I can let go of trying to control (because statement 3) because of _____.

Step 3: Surrendering fixed mindset and opening the mind.

- Can you let go of your attachment to (external validation 1)? Yes -- because it has me stuck at _____.
  - If you answer no, why can't you let go?
  - Now, repeat Step 2 until you can release the small aspects of each validation.

- Can you let go of your attachment to (external validation 2)? Yes -- because it has me stuck at _____.
- Can you let go of your attachment to (external validation 3)? Yes -- because it has me stuck at _____.

Sustaining Internal Validation

Now that you've released the external validations keeping you from living as the highest version of yourself, let's look at identifying and sustaining internal validations.

Step 1: Name the top three internal validations that support you living in the highest version of self.

- Repeat for each validation: When I realize X (fill in the blank with an internal validation) in my life, I feel like I am enough because _____.
- Repeat for each validation: When I realize X (fill in the blank with an internal validation) in my life, I feel like I am capable of achieving it because _____.

Step 2: Accepting love and trust.

- Repeat sequence for each validation: I experience _____ mindset when I believe that I am enough.
  - How did that mindset create love in living as the highest version of yourself?
  - I experience _____ emotions when I believe that I am enough.
  - I experience _____ behaviors when I believe that I am enough.

- Repeat sequence for each validation: I experience _____ mindset when I believe that I am capable.
  - How did that mindset create trust in living as the highest version of yourself?
  - I experience _____ emotions when I believe that I am capable.
  - I experience _____ behaviors when I believe that I am capable.

Step 3: Surrendering & honoring yourself.

Complete these sentences:

- I deserve to use my power and choice to live as the highest version of myself because _____.
- I trust myself because _____.
- I love myself because _____.

Key takeaway

Getting back to the ***real*** you requires releasing attachments to external validation and becoming more driven by internal validation. This chapter continues to underscore the importance of digging up your fear and doubt at the root. Only at the root can you create a more healthy foundation. This chapter also demonstrates that the reason you may struggle to release external validation is because you've lived with it for most of your life. Recognizing how deep this runs should give you much more grace with yourself and insight into why it takes a herculean effort to overturn this dependence. Congratulations for taking a huge chunk out of that step by buying this book and peeling back the layers on this journey. You've determined the source of your validation, how it impacts your life, and how to release your dependence on the validation. You also learned strategies for surrendering to the process of honoring yourself and your truth. For the last five chapters, you've embarked on the process of getting to know the ***real*** you. You dug below the ground to get to the root of your need for external validation and you now have tools to attack it when it comes your way.

You're beginning to understand what a real and healthy version of you looks like without the need to be fed by external validation. Now let's put what you have learned to the test. What happens when you start living as the highest version of yourself and distractions come knocking at your door? How do you remain consistent when life happens?

Chapter 6: Staying consistent and managing distractions

Handling detours is part of the journey

I imagine many of you can relate to this scenario. You have a breakthrough and get unstuck. You start to chip away at your goals, fully committed to a lifestyle change. You're doing your thing for days, weeks, and months at a time then, BOOM, you fall off the wagon. Just like that. Is it *actually* all of a sudden or did you *miss* the warning signs along the way? It is easy to miss the shifts in our mindsets, emotions, and behaviors that give clues that the spirit of defeat is hovering in your mind. The first step is to get curious about what happened versus condemning yourself. Condemnation leads to despair and may prevent your ascent back up. It also clouds your ability to see a way out. *So first and foremost see the fall-off as the task of managing a distraction versus a complete start-over.* It is not a start-over because you have the muscle memory of what you need to do, it is just a matter of bringing it back to the forefront and making adjustments. This chapter is about understanding how to detect and manage distractions so you can stay consistent.

Detecting distractions on your journey

A distraction is anything that takes you away from your intended purpose or the highest version of yourself. They are born from a fear and doubt mindset. Distractions can be good and bad. Meaning that, you can have a distraction that produces good fruit, but it is not connected to living as the highest version of yourself. You can also have distractions that cause harm to your purpose. Harmful distractions relegate you to living less than your capabilities and good distractions create anxiety because they compete with your intended goals. Whether it is a good or harmful distraction, both take you *out of alignment.* Touré Roberts, pastor of the Potter's House at One LA and Denver, and best selling author of *Purpose Awakening* and *Wholeness*, often states, "it is important to pay attention to what the distraction is pulling you away from." Distractions often come when we are on the verge of proving to ourselves that we have what it takes to bring our dream to life. That's when something comes to get us off course to trick us into believing that we do not have the willpower. That "thing" can be a mindset, person, place, or thing that pulls us off course. The "thing" is usually something that brings external validation to fill your tank when you hit an obstacle on your journey. The distraction comes when your internal validation is low and you seek to fill it with a quick fix. Don't fret. This happens to everyone. As Donnie McClurkin sang, "we fall down but we get up, for a saint is just a sinner who fell down and got up." If we know that no one is perfect, then we should have more grace with ourselves when we fall out of alignment. This chapter takes a direct yet graceful approach to helping you figure out the distractions that keep you out of alignment with walking in the highest version of yourself. It also provides tools for staying consistent. Let's look at the distraction that led Amina down a detour on her healthy lifestyle journey.

Amina got detoured

Amina was on a roll, down 50 pounds, working out 4-5 times a week, eating healthy, and maintaining a positive mindset. Things appeared to be going well. Amina's body changed significantly and the weight on the scale dropped. Then, it happened. After great progress, Amina lost the motivation and drive to sustain her peak performance. Amina started to notice the numbers on the scale remained stagnant and she began to feel bored after workouts without the excitement of the weight dropping each week. Rather than dissecting the "why" behind the change in her emotions and mindset or the effectiveness of her routine and the weight loss plateau, Amina started to check in on a few of her out- of-touch mentees. Reengagement led to evenings full of phone calls supporting their needs. As a result, Amina was sleeping in later and later and slicing into her gym time. Reconnecting with her mentees also brought a sense of value and worth to Amina. She felt needed again. Why would Amina compromise her fitness routine by going *out of her way* to support formerly out-of-touch mentees? If you haven't figured it out, she needed validation to numb her feelings of inadequacy from her weight loss plateau. Amina did what most people do when they feel low and do not want to process their emotions. She turned to a distraction that externally validated her to make her feel better and give her a temporary high to relieve the feelings of inadequacy.

Reviewing Amina's story reveals her main source of motivation with maintaining her weight loss journey was external validation: the scale. It could not have come from the internal validation of being healthy or a sense of accomplishment for following a disciplined health regimen, because the moment the scale stopped, so did her discipline. Mentoring others became the distraction that filled her with external validation. Amina's case demonstrates a hard truth: one cannot tie their pursuit of the highest version of themselves to external validation. Doing so makes you susceptible to distractions if you do not get accolades from someone or something. This makes you extremely vulnerable to being knocked out of alignment when things get tough and life hits you. Victory for Amina lies within prioritizing the internal feelings of self- worth that she gets from living in a healthy lifestyle, instead of what she feels when looking at the scale. In order to break the hold of the distraction, Amina must explore the root of her need for external validation from the scale with the 4-step consciousness raising process that we used in Chapter 5. From there, she can build a stronger internal validation system by resetting her health routine, exploring tools for overcoming her weight loss plateau, and transitioning her healthy lifestyle to focus on internal wins. Now let's use the 4-step consciousness raising techniques to identify the distractions that are keeping you from living as the highest version of yourself and build a plan for consistency.

Now, it's your turn

You have a <u>choice</u>: will you feed or resist distractions?

Distractions are inevitably a part of life. However, you get to determine whether you want to invite them to move into your life and draw you away from living as the highest version of yourself. Think about the last time you fell out of alignment with your goals; it is likely that a distraction got you off track. You have to decide to process fear and doubt if you want to stay consistent and minimize distractions. Amina's distraction was the mentees, but for you it could be something else. What do you do when things don't go as planned? Do you make the choice to stop and explore what happened or do you numb your emotions with a distraction?

- Ask yourself: How am I currently using my power to contribute to the emergence of distractions that take me away from living as the highest version of myself?
    - Is your proof of living as the highest version of yourself built on internal validation or external validation?

<u>Presence</u> stops distractions in their tracks

If you paused right now, could you identify the good and harmful distractions keeping you out of alignment with living as the highest version of yourself? Be honest. Noting the behaviors that you didn't realize were distractions brings them into consciousness so you can become more aware of how self-sabotage looks in your lived experience. Pausing to be still in the moment allows you to go deeper.

- Explore the emergence of this distraction: Why is this distraction coming into my life at this time and how does it pull me away from living as the highest version of myself?

Self-awareness helps you understand what feeds your distractions

When you explore the origins of the distractions that emerge on the way to becoming the highest version of yourself, you're able to use specific strategies to address them at the root. Recording the distracting behaviors may provide more granularity for understanding how to interrupt them. This provides deeper insight into the negative impacts of succumbing to distractions. It also helps you identify what you feel is missing that leads you to turn to external validations to numb your emotions. It helps you discern the misalignment that the distraction creates.

- Zero-in on the distractions to identify the root: Are the distractions connected to certain people, contexts, mindsets, emotions, or behaviors in my life?
- Zero-in on ways to maintain consistency: I am most consistent with living as the highest version of myself when I embody _____ mindset _____ emotions and _____ behaviors.

You have to approach living from the highest version of yourself with *intentionality*

Your answers to the 4-step consciousness-raising questions can help you to see how these distractions started, how the footholds became established, and the costs to your overall quality of life. They also help you to see trends that trigger the distraction, or who and what is connected to the distraction. These are all things that can be used to avoid future distractions and create a bounce-back plan. This information alone serves as a powerful tool to snap your behavior back on track when distractions knock on the door again. And trust me, they will be back.

- Put the data to use: Make a bounce back plan for distractions (repeat for each major distraction)
    - In order to address _____ distraction, I need to shift _____ mindset that prompts _____ emotions _____ that lead to _____ behaviors that keep me from living as the highest version of myself.
    - I plan to hold myself accountable to this plan by _____ and checking in with _____ (person) to ensure that I stay consistent with living as the highest version of myself.

Key takeaway

We all stumble. The most important thing is to get back up. Distractions show us the reality of life by testing our discipline to stay the course in the areas of our lives tied to unexplored external validation. Remember you always have the power to choose to be present and use your awareness to make intentional choices. The foundation for rising up begins by choosing to live your life fueled only by internal validation. Be graceful with yourself on this journey as you develop routines and strategies to live as the highest version of yourself.

As you round out this section, you've gained a deeper understanding of how you are using your power. Up to now, you have utilized the 4-step consciousness-raising techniques to identify that:

1. Knowing your defaults and patterns helps you understand the triggers behind the self-sabotage that threatens living from your purpose.

Honoring your light and shadows provides a deeper connection to the *divinity within you* and helps you to live as the highest version of yourself.
2. Identifying and uprooting external validation is the turning point for living as the highest version of yourself. Being able to identify and uproot toxic attachments to external sources lays the foundation for genuine love and belief in your ability to validate yourself.
3. Distractions are a part of life. When they arrive it is a clue that doubt is present and you need to investigate why distractions are pulling you away from living as the highest version of yourself. Staying consistent requires living with intentionality and having a plan for distractions.

For now, let's say bye-bye to distractions. You have a greater understanding of who you really are. You know how to bounce back when the distractions and life pops up. You've uprooted your hidden need for external validation. You are well on your way back home to the **real** you. The next stop on the journey is about believing in the highest version of yourself through a commitment to walking in love and trust.

Accepting: Owning the power within me

"You've always had the power, my dear, you just had to learn it for yourself."

Glinda, The Good Witch, The Wizard of Oz

Chapter 7: Believing in the highest version of yourself

The road back home

You are on the road back home to the ***real*** you. This has been your yellow brick road in your own version of the Wizard of Oz. This is also probably the most honest you've been with yourself in a long time. I'm proud of you. While I can't promise munchkins and witches to join our story, I can promise that you ***are*** making progress on your journey to live unapologetically from love and trust. The key to finding your way home involves using the 4-step consciousness-raising process in a different way than in previous chapters. In Chapters 7 and 8, you'll experience a more in-depth discussion of each step and how it ties into owning your power. You're moving out of problem-solving mode to learn how to sustain the work you've begun. Before we go deep with you, let's adjourn your drive with Amina and Grace as they wrap up their learning journey with a newfound perspective on living from the power within.

Grace owns the power within her

At the end of Chapter 5, we witness Grace starting to unlearn her dependency on external validation and release her fear and doubt mindset. She stopped tying her sense of self-worth to her number of new clients or their affirmations of her coaching abilities. Instead she drew inspiration for continuing in her side business from the sense of personal fulfillment she got when helping others face their fears. She managed to release the root of her dependency on success as a sign of her self-worth and love. As Grace spent more time journaling and asking questions about what's holding her back from leaving her full time job, she realized a hard truth. She cared too much about others' perception of her and that preoccupation controlled her life. She wanted to release this mindset and walk in her full power. Janet, the same friend who motivated her to start the blog, surprised Grace by inviting her to join her Sister Squad coaching group. Six months after Grace began in the group, she reached a turning point. She decided to bring out the ***real*** her and walk in her full power. She put in her resignation at work and is ready to launch her career as a full-time writer and coach.

Amina owns the power within her

In Chapter 6, Amina hit a stumbling block on her weight-loss journey. Although she said she wanted to lose weight and prove to herself that she can maintain a healthy lifestyle, her primary focus was the number on the scale. Amina learned that she needed to turn her focus to building up her internal validation and proving to herself that she can make daily choices that support a healthy lifestyle. Realizing that she needs nurturing too, Amina recently started seeing a therapist who specializes in women who are stuck in the cycle of losing and gaining weight. Since starting her sessions, Amina feels like she's finally letting out the ***real*** version of herself. She started setting boundaries with her family and mentees for how often she can connect with them and support their needs. And she has a better understanding of the emotions that lead her to use food as a comfort. Since starting therapy, Amina is down three dress sizes and is more committed to following her sleep, work, and fitness regimen. To support her commitment to her goals, Amina's family pooled together to buy her a six-month personal training package with a famous local trainer. She's even started to take time to meditate during her lunch break at work. Amina is finally at a place of physical, spiritual, and mental peace and she's ready to walk into her purpose. But first, she plans to let the ***real*** Amina out to her family and mentees by sharing her personal story about her health journey. As Grace and Amina embark on owning the power within, let's turn our focus to you for the remainder of the chapter and the book. Time to own the power within you.

Now It's Your Turn

Make daily <u>choices</u> to walk in love and trust

Activating the power within you requires walking in love and trust and unapologetically owning your identity, brilliance, and expertise. Once you're able to shift away from believing that you are "not enough," you will quench the fire of doubt seeking to overpower your mind, stimulating a mental and spiritual vibration of love. Letting go of the false belief that someone has to give you power means that you trust your voice and the power that's within you.

- How do you want to use your power?

<u>Presence</u> allows love & trust to overpower fear & doubt

Owning your identity, brilliance, and expertise requires making conscious choices on a daily basis. Presence starts with making the intentional choice to trust yourself over the antagonizing voice of doubt. The upside of staying committed to the work that you began over the last six chapters is that fear and doubt no longer have the advantage of your ignorance to power them. You've released the automatic triggers of mindless living by working to uncover the dominating voices, discovered the self-sabotaging mindsets, identified your patterns and defaults, uprooted external validation, gained more internal validation, and learned how to manage distractions. The final step to complete the process is living in presence with love and trust. This way of conscious living honors you and lays the foundation for you to not only recognize your internal power, but also walk in it each day.

- How will you make presence a daily choice?

<u>Self-Awareness</u> fuels the three power sources of love & trust

Being consistent in love and trust hinges on unapologetically owning YOUR identity, brilliance, and expertise. That alone will squash the self-limiting beliefs that pop into your brain on a daily basis and will push you out of fear and into healing and manifestation.

Power source 1: Owning your identity

Identity is always a tricky subject to discuss. It means different things to different people. To some it means background factors like race, socioeconomic status, etc. To others it means culture. To another group, it describes their character traits such as collaborative, kind, and funny. Identity includes each of those factors: background, culture, and your personality traits. Different aspects of your identity matter more or less to you depending on the context. For example, for a Black woman, race may become more top of mind if she is in an all- White environment. Or another person's collaborative nature may take center stage if they're interacting with people who prefer to work alone. The key point here is that you must understand and appreciate the value that your unique identity brings to the world. Too often, we are encouraged to diminish aspects of our identity in order to make others more comfortable. Each time this happens it contributes to a significant loss of internal power because people become afraid of showing the full range of who they are. This means you have to wholly embrace your identity on your own without regard for what society, your parents, or your friends tell you. I realize that what I'm asking of you is bold, but it is important that you not conform to the world. Transform your mind to operate from love and trust versus fear and doubt. When you unapologetically own your identity, you radiate a light that gives others permission to shine in the uniqueness of their identity, too. If you honor your identity, the core of who you are, you set the firm foundation to honor your brilliance.

Power source 2: Owning your brilliance

Embracing your brilliance is essential to manifesting the highest version of yourself. Owning your brilliance means acknowledging that you have intellectual value. The term "brilliance" is no longer just reserved for those with a high iQ or those who people deem as smart. Brilliance is accessible to anyone and everyone who seek to grow their natural gifts and contribute positively to society. Brilliance acknowledges that EVERYONE is brilliant.

When you neglect to own your brilliance you are likely seeing yourself as a small entity versus the *real* you, a person full of power and potential. Each of us carries talents uniquely gifted to us at birth. Only you can deliver those talents in a special way because they are tailored to your personality. Your gifts manifest as brilliance as you discover, hone, and use them. A part of owning the power within you is to share your brilliance with the world. To withhold it (without a valid reason) means that you've relinquished your power in that moment. RESIST the temptation to be sucked back into the old patterns of depending on external validation. You deserve more. The rooms that get the pleasure to be graced by your presence deserve more. Choosing to own your brilliance gives you the stamina to develop expertise.

Power source 3: Owning your expertise

There is a big difference between brilliance and expertise. Expertise emerges when we decide to go *above and beyond* your normal habits and undergo deep study in certain topic areas to be able to *speak with authority* on issues that connect to that content. Brilliance, on the other hand, recognizes that everyone brings intellectual value into the world. We all have expertise in some topic or area that we love. Expertise is not restricted to those with formal education or degrees. One can possess a lot of expertise without going through a formal college degree program. They can gain knowledge from lived experiences, online study, reading books in the content area, certifications, training, or other designations that denote a certain level of knowledge gained that is beyond a novice understanding of the topic. We've all been in situations where we knew how to solve a problem but stayed quiet out of fear when sharing our expertise would have helped solve the problem and save a lot of time, energy, and money. I encourage you to honor your expertise by trusting yourself to speak up. When you hide your expertise, you let fear and doubt win. Sharing your expertise when it is needed is a great gift of love to yourself and others. Doing this embraces your brilliance and your identity as a competent person. The key to all of these core foundations requires embracing the beauty of you.

- How will you reclaim your power by unapologetically owning your identity, brilliance, and expertise?

Intentionally embracing the beauty of you

Embracing your identity as a person full of power and walking in the brilliance of your unique value will help to keep you focused on fostering internal validation. Harnessing the multidimensional power of your identity, brilliance, and expertise can help you cultivate a high level of trust in yourself because you have the damn goods! You didn't become who you are by accident, it is the result of your choices, whether intentional and unintentional. The desire in your heart to live as the highest version of yourself brews within you because you were born to do it. No one else can bring it like you. You did the work to get behind your mindsets and uproot anything standing in the way of your progression. You're ripe to embrace your full self and unapologetically own your place in this world. When you let your light shine, you affirm the belief that the highest version of yourself deserves to live, and you serve humanity by giving others permission to do the same. When you are in the lesser version of yourself, you are not able to embrace the beauty of you.

- Now it's your turn. Identify one specific way you can embrace the beauty of you on a daily basis. Set that as a midday reminder to check in with yourself.

Key takeaway

Everything you need is within you. You simply need to look inward to find your next step for activating the power within you. This power is activated by love and trust and the multidimensional power sources of identity, brilliance, and expertise. The moment you unapologetically embrace those three, you overpower fear and doubt, solidify love and trust, and embrace the beauty of you. When you're able to do that continually, then you're living as the highest version of yourself. Walking in that internally validated self requires consistently releasing attachments to the way things used to be. It requires surrendering to love and trust. The power is always within you. You've completed a full cycle of work to get unstuck. You've proved that you can confront the lesser version of yourself. You know what threatens your progression. You've practiced and implemented the remedies. So what is next? You can either embrace the return of the ***real*** you or stay attached to the old you. Which will you choose?

Chapter 8: Welcoming the real you

Accepting your new beginning

The choice really is yours. You've gone through a complete cycle to reclaim your power by asking yourself tough questions, assessing your answers, and now owning your power. You took my advice from the introduction and responded to the tug-of-war in your head. The ***real*** you is back. It hasn't been easy but you kept showing up. For that you need to commend yourself. I have put you through it. Yet you kept going even when it wasn't easy. Your willingness to stay with it throughout this book demonstrates your ability to activate the power within you.

Your commitment to uncovering the truth means that you are no longer mindlessly trapped in the self-sabotaging cycles. Like Grace and Amina, you've been given the opportunity to reset your self-worth and foster your internal validation. You've been given the tools to unapologetically own your identity, brilliance, and expertise. You have everything that you need to release the fab four of fear (shoulda, coulda, woulda, and can't) and walk in the freedom of using your power to live as the highest version of yourself.

Home rules for the real you

I will repeat the same mantra that I used in every chapter: you always have power and choice in every situation. The golden rule to living from the power within you starts with choosing love and trust as guides in your life. The 4-step consciousness-raising process, choice, presence, self-awareness, and intentionality can help you stop anything that tries to derail you from living as the highest version of yourself.

The *real* you is available to you anytime that you want. Accessing that version of you is a matter of applying these key takeaways.

- Key Takeaway 1: Affirmations and scriptures are great tools yet sometimes we need a little bit more when you have a "stuck order." Ignoring the *divinity within you* aka your spirit's call to live as the highest version of yourself and full potential issues the "stuck order." Using your power and choice to activate the 4-step consciousness-raising techniques enables you to start the process of reclaiming the power within you.
- Key Takeaway 2: The fight for freedom is a spiritual battle of choosing between two voices in your head: love and trust, and fear and doubt. Being more present and intentionally choosing to listen to love and trust over fear and doubt intercepts the autopilot that leads you to live as a lower version of yourself. Gaining a deeper understanding of the fears driving from living as the highest version of yourself is essential. You must use your power and choice to regulate the volume of the competing voices in your mind.
- Key Takeaway 3: You can shift your mindset at any time. You control your power pathway: mindset, emotions, and behaviors. When you feel negative emotions like anxiety and resentment and notice instability in your behaviors, you know that fear and doubt are running your mindset. Use that self-awareness to make the intentional choice to reset your thoughts towards trust by acknowledging that you are enough. That shift is an act of love that resets your power pathway.
- Key Takeaway 4: Personal mastery rests on your ability to live in daily consciousness. It allows you to identify the triggers, defaults, and patterns that lead to distorted perceptions of yourself.

Pursuing personal mastery also helps you to develop intentional strategies to diminish anything that threatens your progression. This knowledge creates the confidence for making intentional choices each day to live as the highest version of yourself.

- Key Takeaway 5: The courage to revisit your upbringing helped you identify the strength of your dependence on external validations in your life. Exposing the miseducation of affection as love provided the foundation for identifying the root of your external validation. Deeply examining the root allows you to replant a healthier foundation of internal validation. Operating from internal validation sets you up for long term joy, success, and peace.
- Key Takeaway 6: We fall down, but we get up. Every time that you succumb to distraction is a signal that an undetected attachment to external validation is present. Uproot both and rise back up into the consistency of living as the highest version of yourself.
- Key Takeaway 7: Believing in the highest version of yourself requires a daily commitment to walking in love and trust and is essential for activating the power within you. Activating the multidimensional power sources of unapologetically owning your identity, brilliance, and expertise demonstrates your commitment to embracing the beauty of you.
- Key Takeaway 8: The ball is officially in your court. You no longer have to only play defense. I've given you the book to play offense and win. Nothing is a mystery. What was hidden has been brought to the light. It is up to you to decide if you want to remain in the shadows or fully come out and shine your light.

Welcoming the real you

Change can be hard, but don't be afraid. Positive change is a part of life. There is freedom in embracing your evolution into a better version of yourself. You've completed an entire cycle of change over the last seven chapters of this book. Now you have to make a ***choice*** about whether to embrace a new beginning and live your life from a lens of love and trust and unapologetically owning your identity, brilliance, and expertise. There is no one like you. You've been uniquely called and gifted to live as the highest version of yourself. This is the truth of the ***present*** moment: the world is waiting for you to live as the highest version of yourself so you can walk in your purpose. No more running. No more hiding. No more shrinking. No more circular unbeliefs playing on repeat in your head. No more dismissing the compliments and words of affirmation from others. No more playing like you are happy and have it all together. No more free reign for distractions to run rampant in your life. No more living to please others at the expense of your physical, mental, and spiritual health. No more living like you don't have any power. Let's be honest about the ***self-awareness*** that led you to this current moment: the tug-of-war in your spirit that made you buy this book. The tug-of-war in your spirit that gave you the courage to complete the exercises. That tug is symbolic of the power within you to reset your course anytime you get off track. It is time to live as the highest version of yourself. It's time to step out on faith and live the life you write about in your journals. That dream is in your heart because God put it in there. You can't run from it. The **intentionality** is in your hands. The tug-of-war in your spirit has called you home and you answered it. Now you can say, **"I live from the power within me."**

Acknowledgements

I am who I am because of the grace and love of God in my life. His words are a lamp to my feet and continually light my path (Jer. 33:3, Psalm 46:5, and 2:112). Thank you, God, for the journey, for bringing me into alignment with your partners as this book came into fruition. Every laugh, every tear, every jump for joy, every prayer, and every depressive moment needed to occur for my purpose. Your love knows no boundaries and that's why you'll always be my first love.

To my mom, Darlene Fisher, thank you for being my biggest cheerleader from day one. All of the little chickadees, hugs, and big bright smiles taught me that I had something special inside of me. Thank you for being my mirror and best friend, every pep talk reminded me of the power within me. Thank you to my dad, Daniel Kwawu who taught me the importance of "exercising patience," that things take time and it is important to honor that process. Thank you for giving me grandma's words that carried me through the hardest moment in my life: "Whatever happens, good or bad, you have to accept it and give everything to the Almighty."

To my brother Anthony, as a little girl, you showed me a beautiful model of what it means to have a big brother that loves and cares for his little sister in an honorable way. I hope to raise my kids to do the same. You are a mighty man and I cannot wait to support your mission to reclaim men from the very streets that *tried* to take your life from you.

To my brother Selasie, although it took many many years for us to meet, I am forever grateful for the continued support and love that you have shown me. I'm so proud of the model that you've set for Naomi on the importance of the father-daughter relationship.

To my many aunts and uncles, grandparents, cousins, "play" cousins, and friends of the family, thank you for loving on me and praying for me. You shaped little Neicey into the woman she is today.

To my belief squad, made up of many friends, colleagues, mentors, and advisors. Thank you for seeing the power within me before I could see it in myself. Lumarie Suders, Valerie Holmes, Larita Anthony, Larry Ebbers, Gay Perez, Marquitta Speller, Lisa Lahey, Ron Heifetz, Deborah Helsing, Anthony Curtis Jr., Tamara Ewing, Lisa Freeman, Tina Tellis, and Ali Fadlallah thank you for the love, prayers, hard conversations, life lessons, and doors that you opened for me to share my gift with the world.

To my spiritual mentors, thank you Deborah Jewell-Sherman for being my rock and light as I entered Harvard and beyond. Now I know *why* God waited to give me my fairy godmother. Melissa Exum, thank you for pouring an abundance of wisdom and power into me before you transitioned to heaven. The lessons I learned sitting in your living room continue to light my path today. Shannon Evette, God led me to your session at Woman Evolve because you were assigned to help me evolve. To all of my pastors, thank you for answering the call, your sermons light my path. Rose Francois, you were God's secret agent, I am glad your sister made you come to the small group table. You've been the spirit-sister and mentor that guided me to recognize the power within me. I can't wait to read your book!

To my editor Sydney Curtis, I brought you a long book with great content and you turned it into a timeless masterpiece that's accessible to all. Thank you for bringing Leslie Weldon to round out the editing team.

To the person scrolling through to the end to find your name, I love you, too, and thank you for allowing me to be a part of our life's journey. May you give yourself permission to live from the power within you.

Appendix

Chapter 5: Validation Test Answer Key
External Validation Responses:

1, 3, 4, 6, 9, 11, 15, 16, 17, 22, 23, 24

Internal Validation Responses:

2, 5, 7, 8, 10, 12, 13, 14, 18, 19, 20, 21

Power and Choice Pathway

You have power and choice in every situation. It's up to you to decide if you want to use them.

The Power Pathway

Glossary of Terms

Consciousness-raising process: the four steps used to create a deeper connection with self that allows you to be more thoughtful about how you interact with yourself and others. The 4-step consciousness-raising process involves choice, presence, self-awareness, and intentionality.

Setting the 4-Step Process in Motion:

1. Choice:
    - Ground yourself with a question: Do I want to use my power to instill love and trust or fear and doubt?
2. Presence:
    - Slow down to check-in with the current moment: How am I currently using my power?
3. Self-Awareness:
    - Assess what's going on within you and outside of you: What's going on in my mindset, behaviors, and emotions that's driving that approach? How is my external environment driving that approach?
4. Intentionality:
    - Make a purposeful choice for how to deploy yourself: Moving forward, how do I want to deploy myself?

Divinity within you: your spirit, a gift from the Creator whose purpose is to sustain alignment with your highest version of yourself.

Fear and doubt: a way of using your power from a deficit perspective that leads to living as the lowest version of yourself. In this state of being, fear torments you and others using your power to fixate on worst-case scenarios. Ultimately leading to doubting oneself and a belief that I am not enough and I am incapable of using my power to accomplish this task.

Highest version of yourself: channeling your power toward love and trust.

Love and trust: a way of using your power from an asset perspective that leads to living as the highest version of yourself. In this state of being, love nurtures your spiritual growth and others by using your power to honor yourself and others. Ultimately leading to trusting yourself and a belief that I am enough and I am capable of using my power to try my "best case" solution to accomplish this task.

Lowest version of yourself: channeling your power towards fear and doubt.

Power: comes from within and you unleash it two ways, internally and externally. Internal power represents how you use your mindset, emotions, and behaviors. You can use them in one of two ways 1) for love and trust toward a higher version of self; or 2) for fear and doubt: toward a lower version of yourself. Externally we can give our power to others in two ways. The first way is by granting someone formal authority to act on our behalf (for example, the power we give to elected officials). The second and more detrimental way is by handing our power over for external validation, so that we can only feel powerful when an external source affirms us.

Real you: feels like a comfortable home because you live as the highest version of yourself. It is the place where your mindset, behaviors, and emotions live in peaceful coexistence. It is the place where you unapologetically own your identity, brilliance, and expertise and empower others to do the same.

Stuck order: illuminates the internal struggle that occurs when you are not paying attention to your inner voice; it is the cry of your spirit to shake you out of stagnation and the cycle of poor, un-affirming choices.

About the Author

Dr. Annice E. Fisher is the CEO and founder of The BEE FREE Woman and Developing Capacity Coaching, LLC. She is a doctoral professor and certified mindset coach teaching individuals and teams how to use conscious leadership as a tool for healing themselves and advancing equity. This work spans across education, business, government, and the non-profit sectors. With more than 15 years of experience leading individuals, teams, and organizations through the change process, Annice serves as a writer and speaker on topics related to gender, leadership, social justice, and mindset. Her work has garnered several awards. She was most recently recognized as an Outstanding Young Alumni Under 40 from the Iowa State University Alumni Association. Annice's writing is a freedom tool for people ready to use their power and choice for change.

Learn more about Dr. Annice E. Fisher's work and download coaching resources: www.beefreewoman.com and www.developcapacity.com.

Follow her online at: @AnniceESpeaks on Instagram and Twitter.

Email Annice to let her know how you've reclaimed your power: info@developcapacity.com.

CPSIA information can be obtained
at www.ICGtesting.com
Printed in the USA
JSHW050133221020
R10429100001B/R104291PG8892JSX1B/1